# A Guide to Jewish Practice

# A Guide to Jewish Practice

*Introduction*

*Attitudes, Values and Beliefs*

Kashrut: *The Jewish Dietary Laws*

Second Edition

BY

David A. Teutsch

produced by the Center for Jewish Ethics
at the Reconstructionist Rabbinical College
in cooperation with the
Reconstructionist Rabbinical Association

**RECONSTRUCTIONIST RABBINICAL COLLEGE PRESS**

Reconstructionist Rabbinical College Press
Wyncote, Pennsylvania



Library of Congress Cataloging-in-Publication Data

Teutsch, David A., 1950-
A guide to Jewish practice / by David A. Teutsch.-- 2nd expanded ed.
p. cm.
Includes index.
ISBN 0-938945-07-6
1. Reconstructionist Judaism. 2. Judaism--Customs and practices. I. Title.
BM197.7.T48 2003
296.7--dc21

2003000251

In Loving Memory of

JONATHAN N. POMERANZ

נתן בן בנימין

The Pomeranz Family

*Table of Contents*

Commentators
8

Preface
9

Introduction
10

Attitudes, Values and Beliefs
15

*Kashrut*: The Jewish Dietary Laws
26

Appendix:
Values-Based Decision Making
49

Index
59

## *Commentators:*

We are indebted to a group of Reconstructionist rabbis and scholars who served as commentators, and whose many valuable suggestions improved the text immeasurably. The initials of individual commentators appear at the end of their commentaries.

Rabbi Fred Dobb
Rabbi Dan Ehrenkrantz
Rabbi Lee Friedlander
Rabbi Richard Hirsh
Dr. Tamar Kamionkowski
Rabbi Amy Klein
Rabbi Jonathan Kligler
Rabbi Myriam Klotz
Rabbi Allan Lehmann
Rabbi Barbara Penzner
Rabbi Linda Potemken
Rabbi Yael Ridberg
Rabbi Brant Rosen
Rabbi Dennis C. Sasso
Rabbi Toba Spitzer
Rabbi Jacob Staub
Rabbi Sheila Weinberg

# *Preface*

This first step in creating a new *Guide to Jewish Practice* rests upon a long history of Reconstructionist thinking about these issues. It responds to inquiries that have been coming from around the movement for years. Sidney Becker, *z"l*, urged that I undertake this project over and again. This booklet fulfills my promise to him.

Special thanks for funding this publication are owed to Jacques Pomeranz, who worked very closely with me and displayed outstanding leadership during his nine years as Chairman of the College's Board of Governors.

The commentators in this booklet are Reconstructionist rabbis and scholars whose views span the breadth of positions within the Reconstructionist movement. In addition to their fine commentary, they have made many valuable suggestions for improving the main text. Final editorial choices and responsibility are my own.

My thanks to Cheryl Plumly and Diane Schwartz, who have typed the manuscript; Chris Bugbee, who worked on design and publication; and Richard Hirsh, who helped conceptualize the project.

# *Guide To Jewish Practice* An Introduction

BY DAVID A. TEUTSCH

JEWS WHO WANT Judaism to play a major role in their lives today need access to inherited Jewish traditions and rituals, values and beliefs. They are interested in shaping their lives by deepening their spirituality, enriching their experience, connecting to the Jewish community, grounding themselves in knowledge of Judaism, and gathering resources for ethical decision-making. Most contemporary Jews do not simply accept the Jewish traditions embodied in *halakha* (Jewish law) and *minhag* (custom). But they want to learn about Jewish traditions and explore in what ways Jewish resources, practices and insights can shape their thinking and influence their values, beliefs and practices. This *Guide* is designed to help Jewish tradition meet Jews where they are while at the same time helping them to be open to the changes and adaptations needed for the renewal of Judaism in our time.

This *Guide* grows out of a tradition of Reconstructionist thought on these issues that can be traced back to a series of articles in the *Reconstructionist* magazine in the fall of 1941 entitled "Towards a Guide to Jewish Ritual Usage." A subsequent pamphlet was revised again in 1962. Since then position papers published by the Reconstructionist movement, guides produced by the Ethics Center of the Reconstructionist Rabbinical College, and articles in the *Reconstructionist* have brought the approach of values-based decisionmaking to a new level. This *Guide* follows that approach to provide a window to a rich and meaningful encounter with the opportunities for Jewish living. It reflects principles developed over the last sixty years:

*1. Unity of purpose, not of procedure.* We share a commitment to divine service, the strengthening of Jewish community, and the pursuit of justice and peace. At the same time, we recognize that Jewish communities and individual Jews will differ regarding how we ought to act. Knowing that we cannot have certainty in these matters, we not only tolerate the fact of diversity; we embrace pluralism as a value.

*2. A focus on the positive.* Our inherited traditions include many *do's* and *don'ts*. In reclaiming ritual, it is valuable to focus first on the opportunities we have for positive observance. With notable exceptions such as eating *hametz* on Passover and work on Shabbat, the *don'ts* can come later.

*3. Not all or nothing.* While our impulse to observe comes out of the Jewish encounter with the divine, the particulars of our practice are the result of complex cultural processes. Especially in ritual matters, an unwillingness to observe everything should not discourage anyone from observing in part. One might light Shabbat candles and still work on Shabbat morning, or shop on Saturday afternoon and still do *havdala*. Moreover, everyone's practice evolves over time.

*4. Reinterpretation and renewal.* Often people stop performing a particular ritual because the apparent reason for it is no longer applicable or appealing. The practice that consequently falls into disuse often has a deeper value that is lost. One example is *kashrut* (Jewish dietary practice), which was abandoned by many because it was a burden erroneously assumed to be nothing more than an outdated health practice rather than an ethical guide to eating designed for its sanctification. Through our reconsideration of the purposes of inherited practices, they can be reinterpreted and renewed.

*5. New circumstances, new responses.* As times change, we need to add practices to reflect changing circumstances and evolving values. Birth rituals for girls, egalitarian divorces and same-sex commitment ceremonies are but three recent examples of these responses.

Our approach reflects the fact that Jewish civilization continually evolves in response to changing social, political, intellectual, techno-scientific and economic conditions. Ever since Jews ceased living in self-governing communities at the end of the Middle Ages, we have lacked the organic community that provided a social and political context for rabbinically determined *halakha*. Our contemporary, voluntary, democratic communities do not have the power to enforce law nor would we want them to, because we have come to value the autonomy of an open society and the democratic processes that accompany it. This places a greater burden upon individuals and communities for determining their own practices. Asking what our ancestors did is not the end of the search, though often it serves as a wonderful beginning.

Rabbi Mordecai Kaplan, founder of the Reconstructionist movement, taught that in our time Jewish tradition "has a vote but not a veto." But giving Jewish tradition a vote is no simple matter. For tradition to vote, we must understand what it says and why. The purpose of this *Guide* is to help readers allow Jewish civilization to cast its vote in their lives. Thus this *Guide* is organized according to times and situations where decisions must be made about personal, familial or communal practice. VOLUME ONE deals with weekdays, including daily religious practice, *kashrut* and general principles of business, family and sexual ethics. VOLUME TWO covers Shabbat and the Jewish holidays. VOLUME THREE examines life-cycle and personal status issues. The volumes are divided into topics and sub-topics, within each of which the relevant Jewish values, ideals, beliefs and norms receive attention. Alternative practices—from ancient to contemporary—are explored in light of these values. The *Guide*'s operating assumption is that each of us weighs and applies values differently so that no two people or communities will necessarily end up following precisely the same practices.

Furthermore, individual decisions about these matters change over time. Some inherited practices, such as *bal tash*h̲*it* (do not destroy, understood also as avoiding waste), have acquired more weight in these environmentally conscious times. Some contemporary values, such as egalitarianism, now play a major role in many of our decisions as well. We value living in an open society and do not see a need to strengthen barriers between the social lives of Jews and non-Jews. The intention of this *Guide* is to explore practices in light of Jewish values so that the reader can make thoughtful choices. Many values have been part of Jewish tradition for thousands of years. Others originate in Western culture and have become Jewish only recently. Once a value is accepted, its origin is of secondary importance.

This *Guide* is intended for use by individuals, rabbis and communities. It is meant both for general study and for use as a reference. A guide rather than a code, it cannot be exhaustive in reviewing the entire *halakha* or in dealing with every situation. For those who want more details of Jewish law, there are many traditional codes available, such as the *Shulhan Arukh*, as well as works produced by other movements such as *Mishneh Berura* (Orthodox), Isaac Klein's *Guide to Jewish Religious Practice* (Conservative) and *American Reform Responsa*. In addition there are now thousands of volumes, many of them in English, dealing with specialized topics at a level of detail impossible in a more encyclopedic work such as this one. Dozens of new specialized volumes are published each year.

While this *Guide* is meant to serve all who will find its approach to Jewish living helpful, its outlook is Reconstructionist: Its position is post-halakhic because we live in a post-halakhic world where Jewish law cannot be enforced. Obligation and spiritual discipline exist without the enforcement of a functioning legal system. Thus we take *halakha* seriously as a source and resource that can shape expectations while not necessarily seeing ourselves as bound by inherited claims of obligation. Therefore the practices advocated in this *Guide* are not monolithic, and the voices of a lively group of commentators provide further insights, arguments and alternative approaches that span the broad range of views advocated by Reconstructionist rabbis and scholars. The *Guide* does not seek to dictate a single approach to practice. Instead, it assumes that thoughtful individuals and committed communities can handle diversity and will of necessity reach their own conclusions.

Because this *Guide* is value-driven, the list of Jewish values that follows this introduction is central to all that follows. While it is impossible to produce a totally comprehensive list, this one includes all the values utilized later in the *Guide*. The list does not include all things we value. For example, we value each *mitzvah*, but *mitzvot* are actions, not values. We value them because they reflect our values. Value-driven decision-making rests upon underlying attitudes and beliefs. We hold many attitudes and beliefs that shape our values, which in turn shape our practices. This *Guide* attempts to identify some of these in order to clarify decision-making by applying the beliefs, values, attitudes, norms, practices, and ideals that provide much of the fabric of our shared experience.

The *Guide* recognizes that it may often be appropriate for community practice to differ from the actions of the individuals in that community. The community is a model for Jewish practice, while the individual is responsible for personally integrating the best of American and Jewish civilization. The community may often be more stringent about an issue like *kashrut* than most—or even all—of its members. Because the community's task is in part to unite its members, its practice should be designed to maximize the comfort of Jews with whom it deals. Thus it might work to accommodate the strictest of its potential members or maintain a high *kashrut* standard in part for the benefit of guests at members' life-cycle events. There would be no inconsistency in a congregation's maintaining a much more traditional posture on an issue of *kashrut* than do its members.

This *Guide* opens the way to experiences of learning and living. It explores the traditions we have inherited, considers their origins and suggests ways of responding to them. A variety of commentators add their voices, and suggestions for new rituals appear. This *Guide* aids in exploring ways to ground personal and communal practice and observance that can make every moment an opportunity for holiness.

# Attitudes, Beliefs & Values Shaping Jewish Practice

*Note: When a value is a traditional Jewish one, the Hebrew name for it is used. When a value (such as democracy) comes out of American Judaism and is more naturally associated with an English term, that is used. When a term (such as commitment to community) represents a traditional value that has been reframed in response to changed circumstances, the choice of terminology will vary based upon what seems most useful.*

***Ahava* (love)** ❧ The gift of love—from parent to child, between lovers and friends, teachers and students—is a central source of joy, nurture and growth, bringing much of what gives life its meaning. Jewish tradition portrays God as the ultimate source of love, embodied in Creation, in Torah and in relationships. Valuing love involves making efforts to sustain and protect loving relationships.

***Anava* (humility)** ❧ Avoiding boastfulness and overconfidence in favor of modesty in self-understanding and self-presentation flows from a recognition of our finitude. This quality does not require self-flagellation or humiliation, but it does encourage cooperation and mutual respect. No one has complete possession of the truth.

***Avadim hayinu bemitzrayim*** ❧ (We were slaves in Egypt [Deuteronomy 6:21]). Having experienced physical and spiritual degradation, Jews believe that this should create empathy with all who are downtrodden, victimized or in pain, and support for them. In the Torah we read, "You shall not oppress a stranger." (Exodus 22:21)

***Avoda* (Service)** ❧ One meaning of *avoda* is service to God. Narrowly, this can be understood as the Temple sacrifices and the worship that replaced them. But the term also refers to work, which can be understood as efforts to improve the world or to contribute to the welfare of society. The early Zionists sang of the redemptive power of work. Our tradition upholds the dignity of honest labor and requires even the wealthiest people to help prepare for Shabbat, because this work provides the context for Shabbat.

***Bal tash'hit*** **(Avoiding waste)** ❧ Material resources are limited, and we have the responsibility to guard against overconsumption and needless waste. No matter how much we can afford to buy, we should protect each thing of worth to any person or creature even if it has little value to us directly. This reflects gratitude for what we have and appreciation for the needs of all.

***B'riyut (Health and wellness)*** ❧ Jewish tradition values the body and good health, supporting measures to protect them. Taking pleasure in the senses and avoiding destructive behavior reflect this value, as does the pursuit of spiritual and emotional health.

***Bitul z'man*** **(Wasting time)** ❧ The minutes and hours of our lives are a precious gift. When we do not use our time well, we squander that gift, which is an irreplaceable resource. *Bitul z'man* is a betrayal of ourselves. We fulfill this value when balancing our efforts to be productive with our awareness of the beauty and miracle in each moment.

***Brit*** **(Covenant)** ❧ The parties in a relationship have obligations to each other. Jewish tradition suggests not only the importance of the Jewish people's commitments to God, but also the covenant made with all humanity and the covenanting among members of the Jewish community.

***B'tzelem Elohim*** **(Human beings are created in the image of God.)** ❧ Because we see ourselves as containing a spark of the divine, we understand every person has infinite worth; therefore, no human being should be treated merely as an object, and we should always attempt to see the humanity in those we encounter. This attitude, drawn from Genesis 1:26, underlies many Jewish values.

***Darkhey shalom* (Paths of peace)** ❧ In a world where tension and conflict so often result in destructive behavior, one concern of which we should remain aware is the need for utilizing emotional, political, and financial resources in ways that create harmony. This especially applies to conflicts between nations, individuals and ethnic and religious groups.

**Democracy** ❧ A value added to Jewish tradition in modern times, the commitment to democracy involves the free expression of opinions and a belief in the ability of groups to govern themselves fairly, responsibly and effectively.

***D'veykut* (Connection to God)** ❧ Awareness of the presence of the Divine in our lives brings the knowledge that our lives are a precious gift. Although we have a small place in an ordered universe, we can be uplifted by living in harmony with the rhythms of the universe and with awareness of the presence of God in our lives. *D'veykut* is thus a life-shaping connection, a much-to-be-desired source and expression of spirituality.

**Diversity** ❧ We benefit from our exposure to different ideas, cultures and ways of being in the world. It is a blessing that the world is diverse. People have differing abilities, interests, concerns and needs that are worthy of our attention and consideration. We value diversity within our communities and in the broader world.

**Egalitarianism** ❧ Rabbinic Judaism recognized the infinite worth of every human life. Contemporary Jews apply that awareness in our commitment to equal political, religious, social and legal treatment for women and men, homosexual and heterosexual, and people of all races and ethnicities. The implications of the idea that we all have been created *b'tzelem Elohim* have growing moral power as current social and economic conditions provide the impetus and insight needed for this ideal to move toward fulfillment.

***Emet* (Truth and integrity)** ❧ Speaking truth to oneself and to others and living in a forthright fashion allow us to create communities characterized by trust, cooperation and mutuality. Living a life guided by pursuit of truth and integrity also removes one of the chief impediments to spirituality and loving relationships. The rabbis said that *emet* is the seal of God.

***Eretz Yisrael* (Land of Israel)** ❧ As the ancient homeland of the Jewish people, the land of Israel has always had special meaning for Jews. With the revitalization of the land, broad-based *aliyah* (migration to Israel) and creation of the modern State, the Jewish attachment to the land has come to mean a commitment to the welfare and safety of the State of Israel as well.

**Fidelity** ❧ Keeping promises and honoring contracts creates a sense of safety and reliability that shapes commercial, communal, and familial relationships in ways that add meaning to work, probity to public life, and warmth and durability to families.

***Haganat hateva* (Environmentalism)** ❧ The natural world—Creation—is a wonder that we are meant to enjoy and appreciate. We are both the beneficiaries of the bounties of nature and the stewards of the natural world. As our power to damage the earth's ecology grows, our ability to benefit from Creation—and perhaps even human survival—depend upon the effectiveness of our stewardship.

***Hesed* (Covenanted caring)** ❧ Loving-kindness in action does not always flow from feelings. *Hesed* is the caring we bring to members of our communities and our families. They deserve caring action when they need it simply because we share the bonds of interpersonal connection. Caring for each other is part of what makes us fully human.

***Hidur mitzvah* (Beautifying Jewish observance)** ❧ Through graceful ritual objects, architecture, and joyous song, wonderful food and beautiful books, we take pleasure in maximizing the attractiveness of our ritual, our moral practice, and our celebrations. This not only enhances our Jewish experience; it draws others to it as well.

***Hodaya* (Gratitude)** ❧ Our lives are a gift. We can never fully earn our opportunities for experiencing love, beauty growth, or joy. They are gifts to us because we were born into this world. It is because even the poorest and least loved of us have received so much that each of us is capable of giving so much back. No matter how much we give, we can never give as much as we have received. Savoring each of these gifts means not living with a bloated sense of entitlement, but instead living a life charged with meaning.

**Inclusion** ❧ Welcoming all into our communities regardless of ability, age, race, sexual orientation, family status or level of knowledge allows our communities to embrace as many people as possible, which strengthens the community while allowing it to full serve all its members.

**Jewish authenticity** ❧ While indiscriminate borrowing from other cultures and religions can undermine Jewish living, Jewish life has been broadened and deepened through what Jews have absorbed from the many cultures to which they have been exposed. Finding the line between enhancement and diminution is a challenging and ongoing task.

***Kavana* (Intention)** ❧ Bringing full attention to our thoughts, actions and words increases the fullness with which we live. Mindfulness helps not only in bringing ourselves to prayer; it helps us live deeply.

***Kedusha* (Holiness)** ❧ Leviticus tells us that God is absolutely holy and that the times, places, and actions that bring us closer to God are holy as well. The system of *mitzvot* is intended to help us become more holy, more fully in touch with the Divine within us and in the world. *Kedusha* has a root meaning of separate, dedicated, or set apart. Particularly in an overwhelmingly secular society, efforts to follow a path of holiness can create life-rhythms that to some extent set one apart from others. We should attempt to maximize the holiness within our daily activities without erecting unnecessary interpersonal barriers.

***Kehila* (Commitment to community)** ❧ According to Jewish tradition, human beings can only fulfill themselves fully in relationship. Community is the locus of our relationships. Furthermore, Judaism as a civilization can be experienced solely in community, can be passed on effectively only through the locus of community. Building and sustaining communities is critical to human fulfillment. As Jews, we strive to create communities that manifest justice, holiness, and peace.

***K'vod hab'riyot* (Human dignity)** ❧ Created *b'tzelem Elohim*, in the image of God, we can see the spark of the Divine in each other. In recognizing that each human face is in part a face of the Divine, we recognize that we are bound to respect the dignity of each human being and act in a way consistent with that dignity. Therefore we should avoid *oshek* (oppression) by, for example, paying workers fairly and on time, and providing safe working conditions.

***Klal Yisrael* (Unity and survival of the Jewish people)** ❧ Despite the schisms that have historically been a part of the Jewish community, the Jews are one people with a shared history. We recognize that we are responsible for each other regardless of differences in ideology and practice, and that since the days of Abraham and Sarah, we have needed each other not only for our own survival but to make the world a better place.

***Ladonay ha'aretz umelo'o* ("The earth and all that is in it belong to God."** [Psalms 24:1]) ❧ We are the beneficiaries of Creation and serve as its stewards. Human beings do not ultimately own what is theirs in the world; it is on loan to us, and we are responsible for doing with it what we believe its owner would will. This key idea underlies Jewish environmental and social ethics.

***Limud torah* (Jewish learning)** ❧ Judaism has a powerfully textual tradition. To understand Jewish civilization requires regular study of our texts not only as an intellectual resource, but also as a stimulus for creativity and an opportunity for moral growth. Text study can create bonds among those who study together, and can be a profoundly spiritual experience that renews and strengthens the student. Study is an integral part of the worship experience and a foundation of Jewish life. Text study includes not only such classics as Bible, Talmud, and Midrash. Poetry, philosophy, mystical texts and current thought are part of it as well.

***Menschlichkeit*** ❧ A mensch is a person of great integrity, courage and sensitivity, honesty and caring. The quality of being a mensch is *menschlichkeit*, which is a Yiddish term. While it has great meaning for Ashkenazic Jews, it should be noted that the Yiddish term was unknown to Sephardic Jews until they encountered it in Israel.

***Menuḇa* (Rest and renewal)** ❧ Stepping back from work, consumption and productive activity for self-renewal and contemplation is a sacred act that provides perspective and offers us an opportunity for healing. This is a major focus of Shabbat.

***Mitzvah* (Obligation)** ❧ Jewish tradition teaches that God gave 613 *mitzvot* in the Torah. While we do not believe that each obligation we have was individually formulated for us by God and we realize that obligations inevitably change over time, we recognize that community can only exist if there are rules that community members follow. A community living in harmony and pursuing the Divine helps its members to discover the transformative power that comes from honoring obligations. Doing what I believe is the right thing simply because it is right helps to create an inner life that is clear as well as interpersonal bonds that are reliable. Some *mitzvot* serve as pathways connecting us to our community and our people, to our highest values, to humanity and to God.

**Physical pleasure** ❧ Our bodies are a gift. We demonstrate our appreciation of that gift by taking pleasure in all our senses. According to one midrash, we will be held accountable for every permitted physical pleasure we pass up—a wonderful meal, a comfortable bed, a walk in a beautiful forest, a loving hug. The *birkhot nehenin* are a large group of blessings that mark these pleasures.

**Pluralism** ❧ In a world where the observance of Judaism cannot be coerced and where groups within the Jewish community disagree about what to believe and how to practice, pluralism is necessary for the Jewish community's survival. In addition, pluralism is critical to democracy, which depends upon freedom of speech. The open exchange of ideas has also been critical to the evolution of Judaism. We embrace pluralism not as a necessary evil but as a source for creating vigor in Jewish life and helping with the improvement of Jewish civilization.

***P'ru ur'vu* (Be fruitful and multiply)** ❧ The first commandment of Genesis is to bear children. While it was originally about guaranteeing that there would be future generations, today the size of each generation is an issue that deserves our scrutiny. The value of nurturing children has to do with the bonds of love between us, our ability to pass on our beliefs, values, attitudes and practice, and the mutually transformative nature of the parent-child relationship. We fulfill this value by raising children, regardless of whether we are biological or adoptive parents. Those who are unable to give birth, or who for personal reasons decide not to raise children, fulfill this value by teaching and providing guidance to young people.

***Rahmanut* (Compassion/Mercy)** ❧ Empathy for those who are less fortunate results in caring action that can involve the emotional, physical, and economic realms. Everyone is less fortunate in some way. All human beings are vulnerable. We need to have compassion on ourselves and others, especially those suffering from emotional, spiritual, physical, and financial difficulties. The Hebrew root of the word *rahmanut* is *rehem,* womb, which implies a deep and abiding love. All who are around us need our caring and compassion.

***Shalshelet hakabbala* (Preserving the chain of tradition)** ❧ The oral and written traditions of the Jewish people stretch back to Abraham and Sarah and beyond. Our inheritance comes from this unbroken chain of living, evolving tradition that shapes our thoughts, actions, and vision. We are the current link in the chain, preserving the extraordinary richness we have inherited and adding our own experience and insight so that we leave a powerful legacy for subsequent generations.

***Sh'lom bayit* (Peace at home)** ❧ If the community is the building block of Jewish civilization, then the family unit has been the building block of the community. Its stability is vital to the community as well as to family members. Those who share daily living should be honored, nurtured and loved by each other. This is necessary for *sh'lom bayit.* When this nurturing is present, the home is a successful primary locus for child-rearing, for building character, and for supporting secure, loving individuals. When it is absent because of abuse or violence or acts of humiliation, *sh'lom bayit* is impossible. Making the home a peaceful place is critical to its ability to carry out these tasks and to bring joy into the lives of the members of the family.

***Sh'mirat haguf* (Protecting the body)** ❧ Our bodies are key to all we can do in the world—and they are a gift to us. Taking care of them allows us to experience and accomplish all else that is important in our lives, to honor that we are created *b'tzelem Elohim.*

***Sh'mirat halashon* (Guarding speech)** ❧ According to Genesis, God created the world through words. Words are our most powerful weapons. What we say can build people up or tear them down, waste time or build relationships, pursue truth or spread rumors. Using words with restraint and wisdom helps to create a safe environment that supports individuals in their growth and the community in its pursuit of holiness.

***Simha* (Joy and celebration)** ❧ Joyously marking Shabbat, holidays, and lifecycle milestones with friends and family, food, drink, and music helps us appreciate what we have, acknowledge transitions in our lives, and make the most of life. Thus Jews toast by saying, "*L'hayim*, to life." The Bible proclaims, "Serve God in joy." (Psalms 100:2)

**Spirituality** ❧ Just as we emphasize the importance of the intellectual, emotional, and physical development of every person, so do we recognize the importance of spiritual development. People vary widely in how they best discover, develop and express their spirituality; we encourage each person's individual development. This might include worship, social activism, meditation, enjoyment of nature, study, and aesthetic experiences. At its best the spiritual life of the community not only strengthens the whole, but it supports the individual spiritual journeys of its members as they repair their souls and seek divine presence in their lives.

***Tikun olam* (Improving the world)** ❧ We live in a world that is far from perfect. Judaism has always had a messianic vision of a world redeemed, a world characterized by justice, sufficiency, harmony and peace. "We cannot expect to complete the task of bringing the world to that ultimate redemption, but we are not at liberty to neglect the task" (Avot 2.16). On the interpersonal, political, and environmental levels, there is an enormous amount to be done, and each good thing we do makes a difference.

***Tza'ar ba'aley hayim* (Prevention of pain to animals)** ❧ Kindness to animals as God's creatures should shape our interactions with them. This applies both to avoiding cruelty (e.g. not teasing them) and to acting kindly (e.g. feeding, staying with or helping a trapped animal).

***Tzedek* (Social justice)** ❧ From Biblical times through the present, we have had a tradition of resisting oppression. To ensure just treatment means preserving human dignity and meeting basic human needs, including education, dignified work, food, clothing and shelter. We live in a just society only when every one of its members is treated justly. Accomplishing that is a shared challenge. Providing funds for that purpose is the act of *tzedaka.*

***Tz'niyut* (Modesty)**. ❧ Maintaining the dignity of others and of oneself and respecting the sacred nature of sexuality involves making thoughtful decisions about how and when to express our sexuality and sexual desire. Modesty also involves not using speech and deed to attract undue attention to oneself. It is equally important for men and women. Dressing appropriately and acting in ways calculated not to attract undue attention help to create an atmosphere of self-respect and trust, safety, confidentiality, and mutuality.

***Yirat Shamayim* (Awe of God)** ❧ Recognizing the awesome Power that unifies the diversity and complexity of the world, the Power that is the source of life, spirituality and ethics, we experience awe and reverence. Humbled by our smallness, we are inspired to reach higher and deeper.

# *Kashrut*: The Jewish Dietary Laws An Introduction

## From *Guide to Jewish Practice, Vol. I*

KASHRUT IS A TERM used most frequently in reference to the system of regulations regarding what foods can be eaten and how they must be prepared. Because it has its roots in the Torah and then evolved for several thousand years, its practices have been hallowed by generations of Jewish use. ✡ *Kashrut*, the noun form of the adjective "kosher," comes from the Hebrew word *kasher*, meaning fit, proper or acceptable for ritual use. *Kashrut* can refer to the specialized rules for Passover food and its preparation (discussed in Volume 2), to issues about wine and other grape-based beverages (discussed at the end of this section), or to whether a ritual object, such as a *tallit* or *tefilin*, is suitable for ritual use (discussed in the sections on each of them). In American slang, something is said to be kosher if it is proper, ethical, and happening the way it is supposed to. Most Jews associate *kashrut* with not eating pork and shellfish, not mixing

✡ **D'RASH:** Rav (a Talmudic rabbi) argues that there is nothing intrinsically pure or impure about certain animals and that searching for a rationale behind the system of *kashrut* is futile. He says: "The commandments were given only to purify people. For what difference does it make to the Holy One whether one ritually slaughters cattle or whether one slaughters cattle by stabbing and eats it? Will such a thing benefit or harm God? Or what difference does it make to God whether one eats unclean or clean substances? It follows that the commandments were given only to purify people." *Midrash Tanhuma, Parashat Shemini.* **T.K.**

milk and meat, and eating only meat from animals slaughtered according to certain rules. But to be understood, these specifics must be seen in the broader context of our relationships to food.

The act of eating involves us at many levels. ✡ Most basically, of course, our lives depend upon the sustenance we derive from the food we eat. ✸ Food preparation, meals and snacking occupy a significant amount of our time and consciousness. No matter how hard we work to grow or purchase food and then to prepare it, we are still beneficiaries of nature and of the actions of others. ✡ Eating becomes a spiritual act when it is accompanied by gratitude for the bounty from which we derive nourishment and pleasure. Eating with others creates an interpersonal connection that at its best is an intimate fellowship. If the food tastes good, eating gives us physical pleasure. Food is one of life's great blessings.

✡ **KAVANAH:** Food deeply nourishes and sustains when converted into energy for the functioning of life. What is your relationship to food and nutrition in your life? What constitute proper, ethical, suitable eating practices for you? What steps do you take to nurture your body through food? **M.K.**

✸ **D'RASH:** Eating is the primary way that human beings interact with the rest of nature. We are composed of the same elements and compounds that make up our food. Indeed, when we eat, we transform a part of nature into energy that we can use for conscious purposes. The system of *kashrut* causes us to pause and consider that while we are part of nature, we are endowed with a unique possibility to make choices in the way we respond to life. **S.W.**

✡ **ETHICS:** Consider the interdependent web of connections in which we live our lives. Take a simple snack, like a chocolate chip cookie made with flour, butter, eggs, cocoa, and sugar. The flour is from wheat, raised and harvested by farmers with the help of whole supporting industries. The butter and eggs come from flesh-and-blood animals who likely suffered as part of the process (though not as much as if meat were served). Cocoa, though tasty, is a notoriously devastating crop because rainforests are felled for cocoa plantations. And the human rights abuses of the sugar industry are well known. Then there are the truck drivers, the packagers and producers and advertisers, the manufacturers of hardware, the refiners of oil, the advocates for more sustainable business practices. The list goes on. How can we be more conscious and more respectful of these interconnections in our daily lives? **F.D.**

Furthermore, most holidays, life-cycle celebrations and family gatherings involve feasting. Eating plays a powerful and multi-dimensional role in our lives. ✡ Our attitudes toward food and eating shape our lives in fundamental ways, so every civilization has its own rules, norms, attitudes and practices surrounding food and eating. Judaism is no exception, and many of its attitudes, beliefs, values and practices about food are embodied in *kashrut*. ✶

From the beginning of the modern era, many apologists have claimed that kosher food is healthier, and that *kashrut* was motivated by health concerns. ✡ Today it is difficult to defend *kashrut* from that position given current conditions of sanitation, refrigeration and government inspection. If there are reasons to maintain *kashrut* today, they are not about health. In truth, the motivation for *kashrut* was never health. ✶ The Torah is explicit that the goal is not sanitation, but

✡ **PRACTICE:** Jewish tradition teaches that whenever two or more break bread and words of Torah pass between them, the *Shekhina* (feminine indwelling Divine presence) rests there (Pirkey Avot 3.3). Food's sacramental function, when combined with social connections, raises the level of meaning exponentially. This is why many Reconstructionist congregations have full *oneg* luncheons following Shabbat services. We come to services not only to face forward in prayer but also to face each other in community, and food enables those connections to be made. **F.D.**

✶ **KAVANAH:** How do we develop and nurture a healthy relationship to food and body image? How do we allow ourselves permission to deeply enjoy what we eat? Developing a personally compelling practice of some form of *kashrut* can help to counter a predominant American cultural attitude which resists seeing our bodies in all of their diverse forms as sacred representations of the Divine Image. Particularly for girls and women in American society, making the practice of food selection, preparation and consumption an act filled with compassionate, grateful awareness is redemptive and healing. Rather than setting ourselves at odds with our desires and appetites to conform to secular cultural norms, we can deeply receive the nourishment we ingest. **M.K.**

✡ **EXPLANATION:** If health concerns were at the root of the Biblical dietary laws, one might expect regulations regarding poisonous and harmful plants as well. **T.K.**

✶ **D'RASH:** Not to *look* better but to *be* better, not merely to become healthier but to become holy—these are the purposes of Jewish dietary laws. **D.C.S.**

sanctification. ✡ ✸ Observing *kashrut* brings holiness and humanity to an act that we have in common with all animals. Primary concerns underlying *kashrut* observance include identification with the Jewish people, creation of sensitivity to the ethical issues surrounding food, and cultivation of an attitude of gratitude and responsibility for the food we eat. ✡

The practice of *kashrut* has developed out of several Biblical statements, so before turning to a review of the values relevant to *kashrut*, key Biblical principles about food will receive attention. ✸ One basic principle is "not eating blood, for blood is the life." (Deuteronomy 12:23) The laws regarding draining blood and salting meat come from this statement. From the statement that "you shall

✡ **EXPLANATION:** The connection between *kashrut* and *kedusha* is made explicit in Leviticus 11:44-45, Leviticus 20:25-26 and Deuteronomy 14:21. **T.K.**

✸ **D'RASH:** All attempts to link eating with holiness are attempts at observing *kashrut* in our day. **D.E.**

✡ **D'RASH:** Another motivation for *kashrut* observance is that it can strengthen one's Jewish spiritual practice. The self-knowledge and self-discipline which keeping kosher requires can facilitate opportunities for reflection on, intimacy with, and mastery over one's physical body in the context of leading a spiritually centered, sanctified life. **M.K.**

✸ **EXPLANATION:** The Biblical system of *kashrut* mirrors God's creation of the world. Just as the world was created through a series of differentiations and categorizations, *kashrut* reminds us that everything has its place in the world. Anthropologist Mary Douglas suggests that clean animals are those which conform to their class, while unclean animals are those which cross boundaries; for example, amphibians live both in land and water and thus confuse the proper order of things (just as the mixing of wool and linen is forbidden). **T.K.**

**EXPLANATION:** The concept that blood holds the life force is a key teaching of Torah. Genesis 9:3-5 tells us that "Every creature that lives shall be yours to eat; as with the green grasses, I give you all these. You must not, however, eat flesh with its life-blood in it. But for your own life-blood I will require a reckoning: I will require it of every beast; of man, too, will I re-quire a reckoning of human life, of every man for that of his fellow man." When Cain kills his brother Abel, it is Abel's blood that cries out to God for justice (Genesis 4:10). Similarly, Leviticus 17 teaches that spilling the blood of an animal is also considered murder unless the blood is ritually drained at an altar site. Deuteronomy 12 adds that if one does not have access to an altar, the animal's blood must be poured into the ground. **T.K.**

not seethe a kid in its mother's milk" (Deuteronomy 14:21) come the rules about separation of milk and meat. ✡ From the law that "you shall not eat anything that dies of itself" comes the restriction that only meat slaughtered according to *kashrut*'s rules may be consumed. ✱ ✡ Biblical lists of animals that are prohibited further restrict what can be consumed; one basic principle is that predators may not be eaten (e.g. Leviticus 11).

Many of these rules are attached to the central imperative, "You shall be holy." (Leviticus 19:2) ✱ The *halakha* has expanded over the centuries to regulate in great detail the rules regarding what can be eaten and when, and in what vessels it may be prepared and served. The *halakha* makes no distinction between the rules for eat-

✡ **D'RASH:** Judaism invites us to locate *kedusha* ("holiness") through the act of making distinctions. Taking our cue from the opening chapter of Genesis, we discover sacred meaning and purpose whenever we attempt to create order out of a seemingly chaotic world. As a result, there are myriad classic dichotomies in Jewish tradition: "Sacred/Mundane," "Light /Darkness," "Shabbat/Weekday," "Kosher/*Treyf*." But why the "Milk/Meat" distinction? Some suggest that it refers back to the most elemental dichotomy of all, namely "Life/Death." Our tradition is in a sense teaching us that if we take life in order to feed ourselves, we should take pains to ensure that the flesh of slaughtered animals is not carelessly mixed together with life-giving milk. By keeping these two powerful symbols separate, we ensure their sacred integrity and endow the mundane act of eating with holy significance. **B.R.**

✱ **EXPLANATION:** Avoiding blood is connected to one of the seven universal "Noahide laws," whose origins lie in the first eleven chapters of Genesis, before the covenant with Abraham and Sarah. Noah's family receives the stipulation that "flesh with its life-blood in it, you may not eat" (9:4). Later generations of Jews understood this law as applicable to all humankind. Even though human bodies are inherently omnivorous, there are moral limits on our consumption of other living beings. **F.D.**

✡ **EXPLANATION:** Rambam (Maimonides) sees Deuteronomy 12:21 as the source of the requirement not to eat anything that is not slaughtered. He associates secular slaughter with sacrificial slaughter. (Sefer Hamitzvot, Aseh 146). **A.L.**

✱ **D'RASH:** Holiness implies distinctions, boundaries, and separations for the sake of sanctification. We need to take care, however, that our concern with holiness-as-separation does not lead us onto the path of separation from our bodies, to the point where we do not taste and enjoy the basic and immediate physicality of eating. Holiness of the body as created in the Divine image is a stance of integration as much as it is of separation. **M.K.**

ing at home and those for eating elsewhere. As is frequently the case with inherited rules, many Jews committed to a form of *kashrut* have modified these particulars. ✡ Thus before exploring the dietary laws in more detail, the values relevant to *kashrut* need to be examined.

Concern for minimizing or avoiding pain to animals (*tza'ar ba'aley hayim*) underlies many regulations regarding kosher slaughtering. ✸✡ This concern might lead some people to become vegetarians. ✸And Genesis suggests the same thing in the Garden of Eden story, where Adam and Eve live in an ideal state as vegetarians. Maimonides, the medieval commentator, made the same point but, recognizing the long history of eating meat embodied in the practice of *kashrut* embedded in the *halakha*, acknowledged that becoming vegetarian is out of the question for most people. From this perspective the laws of *kashrut*, which permit

✡ **ETHICS:** "All or nothing" thinking often leads to paralysis and harsh judgments of ourselves and others. Modifications to our inherited rules are often made because of our values, values which may not have been important to our ancestors. We must determine which values will govern our eating patterns today. **D.E.**

✸ **ETHICS:** Many modern Jews suggest that the veal industry's confinement and mistreatment of young cows should be banned outright as a violation of *tza-'ar ba'aley hayim*. Some go further, asking if any unnecessary killing of an animal can justify the pain and suffering involved. Today, both vegetarians and "deep ecologists" are expanding the Biblical observation that "the fate of humans and the fate of animals are one (as this one dies, so does that one: and all share one lifebreath)." (Ecclesiastes 3:19). **F.D.**

✸ **PRACTICE:** My decision to observe *kashrut* through being vegetarian is influenced by my desire to easily share meals with those who don't observe *kashrut* (not a traditional Jewish value) and to observe the same eating patterns inside and outside my home. Eating in restaurants and others' homes is much easier to do as a vegetarian than as one observing traditional *kashrut*. As a vegetarian, I believe I am observing the essence of *kashrut* even while eating on non-kosher dishes. **D.E.**

✡ **ETHICS:** Some of the critical *tza'ar ba'aley hayim* issues include force-feeding ducks and geese to create *pate de foie gras* (Israel is the world's leading producer), taking day-old calves from their mothers so that they can be raised for veal in very cramped conditions, factory farming and force feeding of cows and chickens that are filled with horrors of their own. **S.W.**

meat to be eaten but only with specific conditions, represent a compromise. That is why some commentators suggest that in messianic days everyone will be a vegetarian.

Some contemporary Jews consciously elect vegetarianism as their form of *kashrut*. This reflects not only a concern with *tza'ar ba'aley hayim*, but also with issues of consumption and concern for the environment (*haganat hateva*) since vegetarians use fewer natural resources. The production of meat consumes many times more resources than producing an equally nutritious amount of vegetarian food, which is of particular concern since resources are so unevenly distributed in our world. ✡ ✶ Vegetarians also have the advantage of needing only one set of dishes and cooking utensils. ✡

> ✡ **ETHICS:** The value of *tikun olam* needs to be highlighted when we consider how many of the world's hungry could be fed if the wealthier meat-eating nations curbed their habit. The planet now has six billion inhabitants and a growing divide between wealthy and hungry. Wouldn't this suggest that vegetarianism is the ethical eating practice of the future? **S.W.**

> ✶ **ETHICS:** A whole pound of tofu has the same environmental impact as just an ounce of beef! Greenhouse gas emission, water table depletion, pesticide use —all are markedly higher for meat than for dairy meals (though dairy and egg products, in turn, are still more environmentally damaging than a vegan diet). **F.D.**

> ✡ **D'RASH:** On the other hand, vegetarianism reduces the specialness of Jews. We are now as likely to bond with other vegetarians as with other Jews. Also by eliminating the separate dishes, pots and utensils and all that entails, there are fewer moments to remember the significance of *kashrut*, to use our eating practice as a call to awareness of our relationship to God, Torah and Israel. We can, however, use our vegetarianism as a form of *kashrut* that connects us to universal values that are also Jewish values and still conforms with the traditions of our ancestors. **S.W.**

Since poultry production is less wasteful than that of beef, pork, or mutton, and since there is less empathy with non-mammals, some Jews compromise by limiting their meat consumption to kosher poultry, which is available in many supermarkets. People with this concern also tend to buy products with a minimum of wasteful packaging (*bal tashhit*). Using environmental concerns when deciding what to eat or consume has become known as eco-*kashrut*, which adds consideration of environmental damage, such as waste and pollution, to traditional concerns. Some people add the working conditions of those involved in food production to the list of eco-*kashrut* issues. ✡ ✸ This is not an entirely new idea. For example, the Va'ad Hakashrut in Boston (the Orthodox organization supervising *kashrut* there) several years ago declared non-union grapes *treyf* in support of a then-struggling effort to improve working conditions for California grape workers.

✡ **D'RASH:** The Jewish mystical tradition understands the body of the human being as a microcosm reflecting the macrocosm of the universe. Conceiving of our personal bodies as reflections of the body of the earth and beyond lends a visceral immediacy to the value of eco-*kashrut.* We are bound up in an organic, delicate, and irrevocable weave of life. The earth and its produce are not ours to master, but rather ours to steward and relate with in nourishing, humble ways that reflect our interdependence. **M.K.**

✸ **EXPLANATION:** A term coined by Reb Zalman Schachter-Shalomi in the mid-1970s, eco-*kashrut* was popularized by Arthur Waskow and the Shalom Center in the late 1980s. Today various Jewish and secular initiatives seek to further the connection by putting an "eco-*hecksher*" on those products which are least environmentally damaging. And eco-*kashrut*'s scope is wider still: today's world "consumes" not only food but paper, energy, land, species, societies. **F.D.**

Another concern related to avoiding waste and maintaining perspective stems from excessively lavish celebrations of life-cycle events and the conspicuous consumption that accompanies them. In addition to the value of *bal tashhit* (not wasting) and that of fair resource distribution (*tzedek*), this can have the effect of having the party overwhelm the significance of a religious occasion, shifting the focus from celebrating a holy moment to partying and eating. In earlier times the poor of the town were invited to every *simha*, an aspiration contemporary Jews demonstrate when they send a percentage of the cost of the party to organizations that feed the hungry such as Mazon—a Jewish Response to Hunger. Decisions about what constitutes a kosher party should entail the careful consideration of all these values.

It is forbidden to eat any part of an animal whose flesh was torn *(taruf)* while it was alive, which is the origin of the word *treyf*, non-kosher. Similarly *halakha* forbids Jews from hunting for meat or fishing for sport, which should also teach a revulsion toward violence. Kosher slaughtering (*shehita*) is done by a specially trained butcher (*shohet*) with a single stroke to the throat of a sharp, smooth blade to minimize the animal's pain. ✡ While contemporary technology allows new humane methods of slaughter, it certainly was a successful effort to minimize pain in a pre-industrialized society. The choice of avoiding non-kosher meat is in part a choice for kindness to animals. Kosher slaughtering meets Muslim *halal* standards, but *halal*-slaughtered meat may not be used in place of kosher meat.

Some Jewish sources see the separation of dairy and meat products, with its origin in not cooking the kid in its mother's milk, as embodying gratitude to milk-giving animals such as the goat and cow. While the Biblical prohibition of mixing milk and meat may have had to do with avoiding the fertility rites of other ancient religions, it is clear that the rabbis used this practice as an opportunity to promote gratitude toward these animals. ✶ The extension of the rule of not cooking the kid in its mother's milk to never mixing dairy and meat was desirable to keep the system simple enough to be observed in a uniform way. ✡ Similarly it was to avoid Jews' confusion about whether it is permitted to eat poultry with milk that the rabbis of the talmudic period classified poultry as meat. The extension of these rules to keeping porous vessels (such as clay pots) for meat separate from those for milk

✡ **ETHICS:** Before refrigeration, it may have been much more practical to chop off and prepare one leg at a time, rather than prepare the meat of an entire animal. Our ancestors recognized this practice was inhumane. Their revulsion to this practice was so strong that the prohibition of eating flesh torn from a live animal is one of the seven Noahide laws (laws incumbent upon both Jews and non-Jews). **D.E.**

✶ **D'RASH:** In addition to promoting gratitude toward animals, the separation of milk and meat stirs us to compassion. It is derived from our respect for the relationship between parent and child. If we are to honor that relationship in the animal world, certainly it might stir us to greater appreciation for that bond of love in our own lives. **S.W.**

✡ **EXPLANATION:** This extension wasn't necessary. Nor did it result in a "simple" system. "Don't cook a kid in its mother's milk" is clear enough. What the rabbis did was to separate eating life-giving substances (dairy) from the life-taking act of eating meat. It is this separation that is at the base of most of the complexities of traditional *kashrut* observance. **D.E.**

came from a time when many dishes and pots were more porous than those now in common use so that odors, flavors and even coloration of food could be transmitted. Thus the laws of *kashrut*, while often complex, are designed to avoid confusion. Of course, the system only has the desired effect if people consider its meaning from time to time.

As noted above, the Torah makes the connection between *kashrut* and *kedusha*, holiness. The life of holiness is one lived with a maximum awareness of the Divine and in harmony with the Divine presence in the world. ✡ In conjunction with the blessings before eating and grace after meals, *kashrut* ideally brings an attitude of gratitude (*hodaya*) and a high level of consciousness to eating. ✸ ✡ While not every Jew who observes *kashrut* always has that attitude, it is an important one to recapture, and keeping kosher pro-

✡ **D'RASH:** So often we run to eat and eat on the run. In this fast-paced world with pervasive fast food, keeping kosher can also be a mechanism for slowing down and noticing what we eat. Even if it is an unconscious connection, when we simply "grab anything" to feed ourselves, we miss an opportunity to acknowledge the relationship between sustenance, nourishment and (Jewish) tradition. When we pause to consider the food we eat, we can engage in conscious eating. **Y.R.**

✸ **EXPLANATION:** Many people have psychological problems around food. For some their relationship to food is symptomatic of their lives being out of balance in some way. Overeating is for some a way of medicating pain, filling the emptiness that is created by the absence of love of self and others. On the other hand, there are those who manifest issues of control and fear of chaos by developing strict regimens of denial around food. There is a growing literature on this subject. Certainly women suffer from the images of beauty that demand intense discipline, denial, and appetite suppression. When we talk about *kedusha*, perhaps we should consider it as the path of balance in life. Maimonides called it the golden way. Judaism does not encourage excess and overindulgence in meeting bodily needs, nor does it promote asceticism and denial of the body. The path of *kedusha* as represented in *kashrut* is a path of self-acceptance and restraint together, a path of honoring the body and dedicating oneself to a set of higher values and greater meaning. **S.W.**

✡ **D'RASH:** Blessings are a way of affirming our respect for, and responsibility to, those divinely inspired natural processes by which we receive our bounty. When we say a blessing, we enter into "right relationship" with the Divine and with the world. As Psalm 24 reminds us, "The Earth and all that fills it are God's." (See Talmud Berakhot 35a-b.) **F.D.**

vides an opportunity for attaining that awareness. ✡ ✸ *Shalshelet hakabala*, the unbroken chain of tradition, consists of a complex mix of ideas and practices, beliefs, attitudes, and customs—a mix that keeping kosher exemplifies.

Since we eat several times a day, *kashrut* is pervasive in the daily living of those who observe it. As a result, it provides ample opportunity for helping children and even adults to learn (*limud Torah*) the values that are embodied in *kashrut*. ✡ As is the case with many ritual observances, people who focus on details may lose track of the broader import of *kashrut*. Minimizing this tendency is a question of how individuals and communities practice and think. A values-driven approach to practice should decrease a focus on details by helping adults to explore their own values in determining their practices.

Shared customs and practices help to hold groups together by cre-

✡ **Kavana:** *(Before eating)* Stop talking, stop moving. In the emptiness of the pause, focus on the food before you. Notice its smells; the colors; the textures. Allow several deep breaths in which you empty your mind of extraneous thoughts. Focus on the gratitude you feel for this food. Visualize its beginnings as raw vegetables, live animals, plants in the earth as you inhale. As you exhale, send a silent prayer of gratitude for the chain of life. Next, think of the people who labored to retrieve this bounty from the earth and send it to the stores and factories. Breathe out gratitude. Breathe in awareness of the people, including yourself if this is the case, who prepared the food before you. Breathe out your gratitude. Next, visualize this food entering your body as you chew, swallow, and digest, converting it to sustaining energy. Breathe out deep gratitude for the gift of life and sustenance. You may choose to recite a Hebrew blessing silently or aloud before eating. **M.K.**

✸ **Kavana:** *(After eating)* Stop talking, stop moving. In this pause of stillness, close your eyes and take in a deep breath, noticing the feeling of fullness and satisfaction in your body. Savor the sensations. Honor the body's digestion process. Silently or aloud, recite or chant a blessing of gratitude for the nourishment you have received, and affirm your desire to transform the freshly received nutrition into life-giving activities and thoughts. **M.K.**

✡ **D'rash:** The fact that we must eat on a daily basis in order to maintain healthy functioning is a profound and humbling daily reminder of our mortality. The personal practice of *kashrut* can help us to respond to our finitude by hallowing the days that are given us as we open ourselves to bless and honor the Eternal, which provides for us in the physical and temporal planes. **M.K.**

ating bonds among the members of the group, differentiating them from others, and clarifying the group's boundaries. Keeping kosher certainly provides that sense of connection and helps Jews to see themselves as a distinctive group. Distinctive practices such as *kashrut* provide structure that plays a critical role in passing on the inner life and values of the culture. ✡ ✸This strengthens Jewish vitality (*klal Yisrael*). One of the hopes many people have in keeping kosher is that every Jew will be able to eat in their homes. Given the array of different standards of *kashrut* and the segments of the Orthodox community that do not even accept each other's *kashrut* as reliable, this is not a fully realizable goal. But it is true that keeping kosher makes it possible for many more Jews—including some who are Orthodox—to eat with each other, creating another tie that links *klal Yisrael*.

Preserving pluralism and building community require the accommodation of both those who keep kosher and those who choose not to do so. ✡ This means that congregations and other Jewish communal institutions ought to have kosher kitchens. This will allow them to welcome

✡ **Ethics:** Jewish women, in particular, as guardians of the home and hearth, are identified with food and *kashrut*. There are negative cultural stereotypes of women using food to exercise power, dole out and withhold love, and invoke guilt. In our egalitarian communities it would be important to attend to these stereotypes and encourage the sharing of responsibilities between the sexes for the supervision and implementation of *kashrut*. **S.W.**

✸ **D'rash:** The Hebrew poet Hayim Nachman Bialik's 1917 essay, "*Halakha* and *Agada*," gives a powerful defense of details. Neither laws nor stories/values will alone suffice; like flower and fruit, they are different stages in a shared cycle. We know that law divorced from values is dangerous and ultimately self-destructive. But what of noble ideas presented without specifics, or enforcement mechanisms (details)? *Kashrut* can be a meaningful practice, but much of the meaning lies in the details. Likewise eco-*kashrut* depends on a detailed understanding of the impact of every action. "The devil is in the details" . . . but so is God. **F.D.**

✡ **Ethics:** *Hakhnasat orhim*, welcoming guests, is a central Jewish practice. Providing a welcoming environment for all who enter the gates of a Jewish institution or home is an essential aspect of Jewish life. Making food accommodations to welcome people from all parts of the Jewish world is thus a practice of *kashrut* that includes emotional and spiritual nurture alongside physical sustenance. **M.K.**

✡ **Ethics:** What is the meaning of a "kosher kitchen?" For me, a kosher kitchen is one in which values inform practice. One of those values is continuity with the Jewish past. Exact observances will vary from place to place. **D.E.**

✸ **Practice:** In my community, even people with kosher homes are only permitted to bring dairy and vegetarian foods to communal celebrations. A vegetarian commitment both reflects a congregational value and keeps our rules simple. **D.E.**

✡ **Ethics:** Depending upon your perspective, eating vegetarian outside of the home may be the "more complete form of *kashrut*." The home observance, which includes meat eating, may be seen as a greater compromise with our values. **D.E.**

those who come through their doors and support their Jewish practice. The desire to support everyone's *kashrut* observance may need to be balanced against other considerations. ✡ For example, many congregations find that having potluck events such as Shabbat dinners helps to build community. Unless everyone in the community keeps kosher or those from non-kosher homes bring in commercially prepared kosher food—which in some communities is expensive, inconvenient, largely unavailable and to some, perhaps demeaning—keeping *kashrut* strictly may undermine the commitment to building community, to celebration, and, where it is difficult to obtain high-quality prepared kosher foods, to *hidur mitzvah*. A solution that many communities have adopted is permitting people with non-kosher homes to bring dairy and vegetarian foods (but not meat) to events sponsored by the congregation or organization in their own building or elsewhere. ✸ ✡ This seems to provide a maximal compromise between traditional *kashrut* standards and a commitment to community unity and celebration. When this is done, the kitchen's dishes and utensils are kept away from the potluck food and dishes so that the kitchen remains available for kosher caterers and for accommodating Jews who observe *halakhically* at community celebrations.

We value our opportunities to socialize with people from many different cultures, travel to distant places, and participate in a broad array of communal activities. We believe we are strengthened by actively living in two civilizations—Jewish and American, for example. Keeping strictly kosher, while not incompatible with living in an open society, certainly makes it much more difficult to do this, so we look for ways to accommodate these values. Many Jews arrive at the compromise of eating dairy and fish in non-kosher homes and restaurants as a way of preserving the essence of *kashrut* without undermining their ability to travel and associate with a broad array of people. Keeping a more complete form of *kashrut* in the home and in Jewish institutions, which are primary locations of Jewish identity, reflects a desire to balance Jewish belonging with participation in an open society.

The description of traditional *kashrut* that follows is designed for homes and synagogues. The values presentation above is intended to provide the lens through which this traditional practice is viewed.

## A Traditional Practice of *Kashrut*

There are many ways to interpret the laws of *kashrut*. The summary of these laws that follows neither attempts to summarize controversies, nor attempts to provide all the intricate legal details. Instead it provides a sufficient overview of the traditional practice of *kashrut* for establishing and maintaining the observance of *kashrut*.

***Separation of milk and meat.*** All kosher edibles are classified into one of three groups:

**DAIRY** (in Yiddish, *milchik*; in Hebrew, *halavi*), which includes any food containing milk or a dairy product such as butter or cheese;

**MEAT** (in Yiddish, *fleishik*; in Hebrew, *basari*), which includes any food that contains any amount of kosher meat; and

**NEUTRAL** (*pareve*), which includes any foods that contain no meat or milk, such as fruits, vegetables, grains, and eggs.

Milk and meat products may not be cooked together or eaten at the same meal, but *pareve* foods may be eaten with either milk or meat products. For example, baked goods served for dessert at the end of a meat meal may not contain sodium caseinate, which is a milk derivative, so usually *pareve* desserts are served after a meat meal. Care must be taken

✡ **Practice:** I often find it more practical to designate certain pots and utensils, especially knives, as *pareve*. Without taking too much space in the crowded kosher kitchen, having a pot for vegetables is less confusing to me than wondering whether the leftovers were cooked side-by-side with meat or dairy. Electrician's tape is sturdy and useful for marking pots and utensils: red for meat, blue for dairy and yellow for *pareve*. **B.P.**

about additives in prepared foods because they are not apparent. For example, some creamers, margarines and toppings that are non-dairy by government standards contain sodium caseinate or other milk derivatives, making them dairy for the purpose of *kashrut*.

Meat and milk dishes, pots, and utensils are kept separate. *Pareve* foods cooked by themselves in a meat pot that has not been used for 24 hours may be served at a dairy meal, and when they are cooked in a dairy pot, they may be served at a meat meal. ✡ This is important to know when you're dealing with left-overs! If this is done, care should be taken not to place a dairy pot or utensil on the table during a meat meal and vice versa. Closed pots cooking on the stove can be in any combination of the three categories, but milk and meat dishes may not be cooked in an oven or microwave at the same time; when foods that have *pareve* ingredients are cooked in an oven alongside milk or meat foods, they become milk or meat.

After eating a *milchik* meal, only the time needed to change a table cloth and clean one's palate must pass before eating meat. After a *fleishik* meal, the time to wait before eating dairy varies by custom. Those of Sephardic or East European descent usually wait six hours; of German descent, three hours; of Dutch descent, 72 minutes. Those who are beginning to keep kosher can select their own *minhag* but are encouraged to follow the dominant custom of their community.

***The Kosher Kitchen.*** The three basic requirements for kosher kitchens are that only kosher foods and utensils are allowed in them, that the meat dishes, pots and utensils are kept separate from the milk ones, and that a kitchen that has been non-kosher must be made kosher (kashered) before it can be used for the preparation of kosher food.

Kashering has several purposes—kashering a non-kosher kitchen, purifying a utensil that has accidentally become non-kosher (e.g. a meat spoon accidentally used for dairy), or kashering for Passover (see Volume Two). When kashering is possible, it is accomplished by immersion in boiling water or exposure to an open flame. Stoves, ovens, refrigerators, freezers, microwaves, counters, tabletops, dishwashers, and glassware can be kashered. Small appliances can be kashered if the parts that have contact with food can be kashered. Any one-piece utensil, pot, or dish can be kashered if it can handle the heat required. ✡ Plastics that melt if boiled, earthenware and unglazed pottery (because it is too porous to be purged), utensils with handles of another material (because foreign substances can get trapped between the two materials) and porcelain cannot be kashered, but if they have substantial worth and are put aside for a year, they are considered new and can be used. ✸

✡ **PRACTICE:** Some oven-proof ceramics cannot be kashered (e.g. pottery), some can be kashered by immersion (Corningware, Corelle), and others need simple washing (Pyrex). **A.L.**

✸ **PRACTICE:** Most interpreters of traditional *kashrut* do not accept the rabbinic opinion that expensive dishes and utensils can become kosher if they are stored for a year. **A.L.**

✡ **PRACTICE:** Certain cooking and eating utensils are porous. With heat, food substances can meld with the utensils. The principle behind kashering is that food substances which have entered the utensils should now be removed. The way to remove them is the same as the way they entered in the first place, through heat. **D.E.**

✸ **D'RASH:** Whether kashering a home for the first time or in the annual Pesah preparations, I find the dramatic use of flame and hot water a powerful cleansing ritual for this awesome change. When moving into a new home, I took pride in using a blowtorch to *kasher* the oven and consecrate it for our holy use. After a kitchen has been renovated is an ideal time to consider transforming a home into a kosher home. **B.P.**

When an article is kashered, it must first be completely cleaned. Then it is left unused for 24 hours. When possible, the article is then immersed in boiling water. At the least, it must be brought to a temperature higher than the one at which it was made non-kosher. ✡ A large pot can be kashered by filling it to overflowing with boiling water (Sometimes the overflowing is caused by dropping in a red-hot stone). ✸ To *kasher* a microwave, a glass of water is placed in it, brought to a boil and kept boil-

✡ **Practice:** Out of concern for natural resources (*haganat hateva*) and avoiding waste (*bal tashhit*), I have concluded that the requirement to run an extra rinse cycle no longer holds water. **B.P.**

ing for several minutes; the steam purges the microwave. After cleaning, a stove is turned to its highest setting and allowed to glow. An oven is put through a self-cleaning cycle if it has one; if not, once cleaned, it is left on its highest setting until the oven reaches that temperature. Refrigerators, freezers, and glass (including non-porous ovenproof ceramics) are kashered simply by thorough washing. Countertops must be thoroughly scoured, allowed to sit for 24 hours, and then covered with boiling water.

Glassware, Pyrex and other non-porous ovenproof ceramics are considered *pareve* (neither dairy nor meat) when they are clean. Separate dairy and meat sections of the kitchen are used for storage. Meat and dairy utensils cannot be washed together. Separate sponges, scouring pads, washcloths, washtubs, and drying racks are used for milk and meat. Milk and meat may not be in the dishwasher at the same time. If the same machine is used for both, dishes must be rinsed thoroughly before placing them in the dishwasher, and a rinse cycle must be run between using the dishwasher for milk and for meat. ✡

If a bit of meat should accidentally fall into dairy food or vice versa, and if it comprises less than one part in sixty (*batel beshishim*), and if it does not substantially alter the food, then the food is not made non-kosher, and the vessels do not have to be kashered. The same is true if a non-kosher substance should fall in.

***Permitted Foods.*** Fresh fruits, vegetables, grains, sugar, and pure spices are kosher and do not require rabbinic supervision (*hashgaha*). Canned and frozen fruits and vegetables that have only spices added are also kosher, but ingredients must be read carefully to insure that they have no other additives; particular caution is needed to ensure that a product is not *milchik* if it is to be eaten with a meat meal. Eggs are kosher and do not require supervision, but an egg with a speck of blood in it is *treyf.*

Milk, butter, cottage and cream cheese, and hard cheeses (which are made with a dry, powdered rennet) are also kosher without requiring rabbinic supervision. However, such soft cheeses as roquefort, brie, and blue cheese can be made using fresh rennet from a non-kosher source, so these require a *heksher* (certification of rabbinic supervision). ✡ If rennet comes from a non-kosher source that could have been eaten (e.g. a piece of stomach), the cheese is not kosher, but if the rennet is an animal secretion that would not be eaten on its own (*pirsa b'alma*), then it does not prevent the cheese from being kosher. The additives in cheese can also be non-kosher.

✡ **PRACTICE:** Rennet is manufactured in the United States by drying the stomach (*yavesh k'eytz* / dry as wood) extracting the active enzyme (*lo ra'uwi la'akhilat kelev* / unfit for a dog to eat), and then redrying (*k'even* / like a stone), which leaves it kosher and *pareve*. But cheese is a processed food containing other additives, so it needs rabbinic supervision. **A.L.**

✸ **EXPLANATION:** An understanding of *kashrut* as a symbol system was first articulated by Philo of Alexandria, who, under the influence of Greek philosophy, looked for symbols embedded within the specific regulations. For example, he argued that fins and scales were signs of endurance and self control and that the consumption of fish with fins and scales would transmit these qualities to the human soul. **T.K.**

Fish with fins and scales are kosher and *pareve*. ✸ These include anchovies, bass, bluefish, bluegill, carp, char, cod, crappie, dolphinfish (but not dolphin, which is a mammal), drums, flounder, haddock, halibut, herring, mackerel, mahimahi, perch, pike, plaice, pollock, pompano, redfish, salmon, sardines, sea bass, seatrout, smelts, snapper, sole, sturgeon, sunfish, swordfish, tilapia, tilefish, trout, tuna, turbot, whitefish, whiting and yellowtail. Caviar from kosher fish is kosher. Non-kosher fish include all kinds of shellfish (e.g. abalone, clams, crab, crayfish, lobster, mussels, oysters, scallops, shrimp) angles, blowfish, bullfish, catfish, eel, gars, lumpfish, monkfish, rays, and sharks. Whales, dolphins and porpoises are non-kosher mammals.

Meat from animals that have cloven hooves and chew their cud is kosher provided that it has a *heksher*. Meat from cattle (beef and veal), sheep (mutton and lamb), goats, buffalo, and deer is kosher if the animal was slaughtered according to the rules of *shehita* and the meat has a *hekshe*r. ✡ Meat from pigs, ✸ hogs, rabbits, squirrels and carnivores is never kosher.

Kosher fowl include capon, chickens, cornish hens, doves, ducks, geese, partridges, peacocks, pheasant, pigeons, quail, squab, and turkeys. These must be kosher-slaughtered and must bear a *hekshe*r; fowl is a kind of meat. Kosher butchers carry beef, veal, chicken and turkey; duck, lamb, and Cornish hens are not uncommon.

Before meat and poultry can be consumed, they must be slaughtered according to the rules of *she<u>h</u>ita*, which ensure a relatively painless death and the complete draining of blood. Once this is done, various organs are inspected to ensure there are no defects. The designation *glatt* kosher means that the lungs are not only as smooth as they need to be for *kashrut*; ✡ they are perfectly smooth. This standard is beyond what is required; those who adhere to it are being very strict (*ma<u>h</u>mir*). The sciatic nerve of cattle and sheep may not be eaten; because it is difficult and expensive to remove, most kosher meat in the U.S. does not come from the hindquarters. ✸

✡ **Explanation:** The distinction between pure and impure animals first occurs in the Flood story in Genesis. According to one Biblical tradition (known as the Changeable source), Noah was commanded to bring seven pairs of pure animals and two pairs of impure animals into the ark. However, another tradition embedded in the Biblical text (known as the Priestly source) suggests that Noah brought two pairs of every animal into the ark. This latter tradition represents the opinion that *kashrut* was first ordained at Sinai, while the former tradition imposes a system of *kashrut* for all humanity (Noahide laws). **T.K.**

✸ **Explanation:** The pig receives so much attention because it is a borderline case. It is a domesticated land animal with a fully cleft hoof, but it does not chew its cud. **T.K.**

✡ **Explanation:** Smooth (Yiddish *glat*) lungs are unquestionably kosher, perforated lungs are definitely unkosher, and lungs with healed-over perforations raise questions which need to be resolved before the *kashrut* of the animal can be determined. Some classic codifiers were stricter here (R. Yosef Karo) than others (R. Moses Isserles). Glatt Kosher meat comes from animals whose lungs weren't at all suspect. **A.L.**

✡ **Explanation:** When Jacob wrestled with the angel/man, he was wounded in his sciatic nerve. The Torah prohibits eating the sciatic nerve as a way of reminding us of this story. Through our observance, we allow the story of Jacob to affect our behavior. *Ma'aseh avot siman l'banim* (the deeds of the patriarchs and matriarchs are re-lived in the lives of their children). **D.E.**

Kosher meat must be soaked and salted or broiled to eliminate any remaining blood. This must be done before meat is frozen, so if the consumer buys it frozen, the consumer should make certain that it has already been salted. Some kosher butchers routinely salt meat before they sell it. Others do it on request. ✡ When purchasing meat from a new butcher, it is advisable to inquire. If salting is done at home, the meat is soaked for a half-hour in a tub reserved for that purpose. After being drained on an angled surface, it is covered in coarse salt (usually sold as kosher salt) for an hour. ✸ Poultry must be drained with the cavity downward and salted inside and out. After salting, the meat is rinsed three times. Special procedures using less salt or substituting potassium chloride are available for those on low-salt diets for medical reasons. Because liver is so rich in blood, it is always scored with a sharp knife and broiled after light salting instead of using the regular salting procedure. Other kinds of meat may also be broiled instead of salted. Broiling can be done in a gas or electric broiler, in an oven designed for broiling, or on a barbecue. Ground or chopped meat should be kashered before it is ground.

✡ **PRACTICE:** The purchase of approved kosher food, including the validation of butchers and bakers, can be fraught with political and moral issues. At times I have chosen to support a Jewish business when it was denied certification only because of a financial or other disagreement. Likewise, a business that follows *kashrut* meticulously but has acted unethically in its dealings with the public or its workers has lost our family's support. **B.P.**

✸ **D'RASH:** I have childhood memories of seeing a slab of meat or chicken on the white metal drain board slanted toward the sink in the kitchen. Right nearby was the red and yellow box of Diamond Kosher Salt. It was a common sight. I took it for granted. I noticed how the pinkish liquid dripped into the sink and how my mother rinsed the flesh again and again. Is it true that somehow, something was transmitted in that scene? Could it be an antipathy to bloodshed and violence, a desire for peace, a love of life? **S.W.**

***Processed Foods.*** It is difficult to determine the ; of processed foods. If a product contains meat or a meat derivative and is not certified kosher, it is not. If it has "shortening" as an ingredient, it probably has animal fats in the shortening unless it specifically says "vegetable shortening." Dairy additives include whey, lactose, and casein. Gelatin and chemical rennet are considered kosher by us because of the way they are processed (creating something new, *davar hadash*). Because checking for the *kashrut* of processed foods by reading ingredients is difficult, the only way to achieve full certainty of the *kashrut* of processed foods is to purchase only those that are certified kosher. ✡ This is true of baked goods as well, where ingredients and vessels are an issue, as is the question of what is *pareve* and what is *milchik*. Most Jews who keep kosher do rely on careful reading of labels, which in the United States are regulated by the government. Because the accuracy of labels depends upon government regulations and their enforcement, label reading as a method of determining *kashrut* is completely unreliable in many parts of the world.

✡ **Practice:** Habitual label reading creates a familiarity with the ingredients of the foods we eat. Personally, I prefer to rely on my own label reading and self-imposed standards of *kashrut* rather than allow a rabbinic collective to make *kashrut* determinations for me. **D.E.**

***Kosher Certification.*** There are dozens of reliable sources of *hashgaha* available. They appear on many products. Among the most common are:

 Joint Kashruth Commission, Union of Orthodox Jewish Congregations of America

 Organized Kashruth Laboratories

 Council of Orthodox Rabbis.

 Kosher Supervision Service of New Jersey

 Kashruth Commission of the Associated Synagogues of Massachusetts

 Kosher Overseers Association of America

When a product has a K on it, that indicates someone believes it to be kosher, but only investigation will indicate who has made that judgment and whether it can be relied upon. When a P appears alongside the *hekshe*r on a product, it usually means that it is acceptable for Passover use; it is NOT an indication that the product is *pareve*. A D alongside the *hekshe*r indicates that the *mashgiah* (person certifying the *kashrut* of the product) believes it to be dairy.

***Wine.*** There are two issues regarding wine. The first is its ingredients. ✡ Several authorities have ruled that all wine has kosher ingredients. Others say that some foreign wines have additives that are suspect. The second issue is that Jews are traditionally forbidden to drink the wine of idolators (*Yayin nesekh*). This was originally an effort to keep Jews from drinking libations to the gods, a practice no longer in use, and later to minimize contact between Jews and non-Jews. These concerns clash with our values. We now hold that all wine is simply wine (*stam yeynam*). ✸ Kosher-certified wine is needed only on Passover, when there is concern about leavening (*hametz*). However, some Jews prefer to make *kiddush* over wine from Israel to indicate our connection to *Eretz Yisrael*. ✡ The same rules as those for wine apply to brandy, cognac, and grape-based liqueurs. All beer, whiskey and other pure spirits are kosher without a *hekshe*r except on Passover.

✡ **PRACTICE:** Recent investigation has indicated that "fining agents" added to wine may include dairy or meat products, making use of wine with a rabbinic *hekshe*r advisable. **A.L.**

✸ **PRACTICE:** Traditionally, any wine that was touched by a non-Jew became non-kosher. The Conservative Law Committee determined that today, since wine is made through automated processes that avoid direct contact with people, all wine is potentially kosher. The reasoning of the Conservative Law Committee maintains a respect for the traditional ruling, which I do not share. I consider all wine kosher because I object in principle to interfering with social contact between Jews and non-Jews. **D.E.**

✡ **PRACTICE:** I encourage the use of kosher wine in Jewish ritual from kiddush on Shabbat and *hagim* to weddings and other *simhas*, and especially encourage people to taste and discover the wide variety of fine kosher wines available today. **B.P.**

## Conclusion

Vegetarianism, eco-*kashrut* and traditional *kashrut* represent three values-driven approaches to conscious eating. While different values are associated with each of them, all three are compatible with each other. One can observe any combination of them that reflects one's moral, spiritual, and Jewish concerns. ✡ While people's choices may change over time, they should always serve to enhance gratitude, sensitivity to ethical issues, responsibility regarding the consequences of our choices and connection to the Jewish people. Thus *kashrut* should help us to encounter daily the moral and spiritual dimensions of eating.

✡ **D'RASH:** Living in harmony with the Divine presence in the world is an important goal for every Jew, whether or not one chooses to keep kosher in a traditional way. In a society in which the majority of the food on supermarket shelves is either unhealthy, unnecessary, or produced by a vast corporation with little concern for sustainable living, choosing to eat in a way that acknowledges both our own bodies' true needs and an awareness of the impact of our consumption on others is a truly holy act. Eating in this way might mean making a decision not to harm animals, to support local farmers and food producers, to spend the time and money necessary to honor our bodies and eat in a healthy way, or not to buy food that's wrapped in excessive packaging. The fundamental teaching and challenge of the tradition of *kashrut* is that what we put in our mouths and how it gets there matters. The rest, to some extent, is commentary. **T.S.**

# *Appendix* Values-Based Decision Making

VALUES-BASED DECISION MAKING has become a catch-phrase in Reconstructionist circles, reflecting a desire to develop an orderly and valid process for individuals and groups to decide upon their policies, procedures and behavior. The need for a system as self-consciously considered as values-based decision making grows out of several realities. Most Jews no longer consider themselves to be bound by *halakha*, and will not simply accept the opinion of a rabbi. Indeed most liberal rabbis do not consider themselves bound by the decisions of the rabbis' rabbi. Furthermore, most Jews know they are living in a society that does not reflect an ethical orientation with which they fully agree. The two most obvious ideologies in America today are those of the Christian Right and the materialistic hedonism purveyed by the media and advertising. Most Jews are seeking an approach closer to their own moral outlook, an outlook partly shaped by their Jewish backgrounds. Values-based decision making provides a way of thinking through and expressing our commitments, allowing us to create ground to stand on somewhere between the *halakha* and the *New York Times*. It has been used within the Reconstructionist movement for 20 years and is most recently embodied in this *Guide to Jewish Practice*.

## *Decision-Making Process*

Many of those who talk about values-based decision making, however, do not recognize that it involves the application of many other criteria besides values alone. In fact, employing values occurs nearly at

This essay was first published in *The Reconstructionist*, Vol. 65, No. 2.

the end of a values-based decision making process. A typical values-based decision making process contains the following steps:

1. Determine facts, alternative actions and their outcomes.
2. Examine relevant scientific and social scientific approaches to understanding these.
3. Consider the historical and contemporary context, including the history and rationales of Jewish practice.
4. Look for norms that might exclude some actions.
5. Assemble and weigh relevant attitudes, beliefs and values.
6. Formulate decision alternatives.
7. Seek consensus (if a group is deciding).
8. Make the decision.

Values-based decision making has its roots in the British-American tradition of moral philosophy that sees our lives as subject to a complex series of facts and concerns that cannot be reduced to a few very broad principles from which everything else can be deduced. One example of the broad-principle approach is the work of Immanuel Kant and such successors as John Rawls. The Kantian school attempts to derive all conduct from such principles as the categorical imperative, which states that we should only do things that would benefit people if everyone did them. Other people use the Golden Rule ("Do unto others...") as a broad principle. One problem with moral philosophies that derive ethical systems from just a few core principles is that they do not capture the richness and complexity of most people's moral concerns. How do I apply the Golden Rule, for example, to the question of euthanasia for someone whose beliefs and values are totally different from my own? For a decision-making system to work in real life, it must work in a cultural context that reflects the thicket of our moral experience, which is a tangle of beliefs and attitudes, rights and norms, obligations, values and practices.

## *First Principles*

Systems that start from a few basic principles (sometimes called "first principles") are difficult to interpret and apply—fatal flaws if non-philosophers are to use them. When we apply the Golden Rule to end-of-life issues, we need to explore what we want for ourselves, and why and how the other person differs in what that person would want and why. Then we would need criteria for exploring the legitimacy of these distinctions in values, attitudes and practices. We would also need to weigh how all this should affect the application of the Golden Rule.

For example, a Catholic believes that only God should take a life. If I disagree, how does that affect the decision I need to make regarding that person? Clearly the outcomes in different cases will vary person to person because considerations far beyond the Golden Rule would have to be brought to bear. As for euthanasia, applying the Golden Rule usually involves many other moral considerations which shape the decision maker's thinking whether or not that person is conscious of it. Unless these moral considerations are examined in their full complexity, the legitimacy of the conclusion is undermined.

## *Understanding the Context*

Values-based decision making takes for granted that good decisions reflect consideration of the context in which they are made. That context is made up of political, economic, social, and techno-scientific factors over which individuals and small groups often have little control. The context is also cultural in the broad sense (e.g. American, Jewish, Reconstructionist) and in the narrow sense (the culture of a congregation, family, or organization; the web of such cultures within which an individual lives).

Sometimes people divide decisions into moral ones and ritual ones. But virtually all decisions have a moral component. For example the decision about whether to keep kosher, and if so, where and how, raises issues that touch on ecology, kindness to animals, and the centrality of Jewish community. So while issues and decisions may also have aesthetic and prudential components that are not moral, they virtually always have a moral component as well. The decision-making method can stay largely the same.

Thus the best approach to food distribution in a drought-stricken African nation with poor transportation and communication systems will differ considerably from the best method in an American city. This illustrates that the moral dimension to decisions exists alongside an array of prudential concerns. These prudential concerns need to be clarified at the first stage of values-based decision making because they provide the required context for decision making. Determining the facts, possible courses of action, and their costs and consequences provides knowledge needed to make ethical decisions. Skipping this step often creates acrimony and confusion.

Once the facts and consequences underlying a major decision have been established, it is helpful to employ the insights of relevant academic disciplines. Depending on the decision, this might entail considering the issues from the perspectives of anthropology, medicine, psychology, the sciences and other fields. This process is likely not only to shape the understanding of the decision maker. It will often help in the discovery of unselfconsciously held beliefs and assumptions that shape decision making. Those beliefs and assumptions might be about human nature, or expected community conduct, or the reliability of information or commitment-based action, or dozens of other areas.

## *Universal and Particular*

All of this information must be placed in its cultural context. We don't make decisions that are valid for all people in all places. We make decisions that are sensible for a certain time, place, and group of people. But aren't there some rules that are universal? It may be true that under some circumstances one can legitimately kill—for example, in self-defense—but isn't it the case that one should never murder? Jewish tradition accepts this as a universal rule, which is what a norm is. Such norms require some actions and forbid others, and they guide us at the extremes of conduct. The Ten Commandments contains many norms. values-based decision making only operates away from these extremes because our conduct at the extremes is regulated by norms. In other words, values-based decision making operates within the areas not determined by norms.

These norms operate in consonance with our underlying attitudes. For example, one fundamental Jewish teaching is that human beings are created *b'tzelem Elohim*, in the image of God. That supports the belief that each of us has infinite worth. This belief supports the norm that forbids murder. The attitudes and beliefs we have also support our values.

## *Moral Building Blocks*

When our attitudes, beliefs, norms, values and practices are in harmony with each other, they are mutually reinforcing. Since we often absorb these moral building blocks unselfconsciously, absorbing one of these elements does not always precede the others in time. While we might understand some of them as being more fundamental than others, each of them depends on the others for creating moral lives of substance. Even our understanding of virtues is interactive with the other moral elements.

*Menschlichkeit*, for example, is a peculiarly Jewish virtue that reflects many of our values and beliefs. It includes such other virtues as honesty, courage, and compassion, which in turn tie to our vision of a just and caring society. The Reconstructionist understanding of our civilization as evolving and of our sacred texts as emerging from their historical contexts contributes to the possibility of linking our contemporary moral sensibilities with our encounters with Jewish texts and traditions. This helps us integrate our theological language, experience, and morality. This is critical if we as a minority group are to sustain our moral practice.

The very idea of values, of "value," comes from our consciousness that the world is God's (I would prefer to say that the world is infused with the divine); that the world has worth is one corollary of that attitude. What we recognize as having worth is at best consistent with our attitudes, but our attitudes cannot fully predict our values. Our values grow out of our experiences and cultures. The attitude *Ladonay ha'aretz umlo'o* ("The world and all that is in it belongs to God"—Psalm 24) means that everything in the world has the capacity for good, but this insight has to be fleshed out by values before we can easily act on it.

## *Beliefs and Assumptions*

We cannot make decisions wisely unless we are aware of what shapes those decisions. Our beliefs about the right balance between community responsibility and individual autonomy are so powerful in shaping decisions that they need careful examination to ensure that the balance between those beliefs is the one we consciously mean to apply. Often decision making goes awry because people are not aware of how their beliefs and assumptions drive their conclusions. When beliefs and assumptions are not articulated, dialogue often generates more heat than light, and individual decision making becomes erratic and confused. Once made explicit, beliefs and assumptions can be tested against knowledge and experience, creating a more rational and orderly universe of discourse.

Assuming we have clarified the facts and scholarship relevant to a decision and that the decision is not completely determined by norms, we next will need to understand its context in past history and practice as well as in contemporary culture. Understanding our predecessors' practices and what motivated them helps us to explore our own attitudes, beliefs, norms, and values. Empathetic consideration of our heritage gives Judaism a vote. Having done this, we can turn to exploring the rest of the values relevant to a decision.

Each decision that we make has a moral component to which values can be applied, but each decision is also affected by different values. Even when two decisions are shaped by similar values, some values will be more central to one decision than the other. Once we are at the values stage, it is time to consider which values are more important and, in light of all the previous steps in the decision-making process, why. Some values have a more direct connection to a particular issue, and some are felt more strongly. The history of values and their origin affects the weighting of values as well. The value of community is far more central to deciding whether to attend a shiva minyan than it is to how expensive a cut of meat to buy.

Applying that emerging hierarchy of values to the decision and its consequences prepares the decision maker to select the best—or sometimes the least bad—choice. Thus in values-based decision making, exploring values is the last step in the process before actually making the decision.

## *Who Decides?*

When groups need to make a decision, they should begin by seeking agreement about who ought to make it. Decisions can most efficiently be made by the smallest group with sufficient authority and competence to make them. Sometimes a series of groups needs to be involved; in a synagogue, a membership or ritual committee decision of importance might require board approval. If the issue is fundamental enough, the board might seek ratification by the congregation's members. Critical to the legitimation of the decision is the broad affirmation in advance of the legitimacy of the process and the decision-making group. Groups' decision making therefore needs to be carefully planned. If the process is affirmed in advance (in part because those who care will have sufficient input to satisfy them) the outcome of the process will usually be accepted by those who disagree with it.

At the group level where the recommendation is formulated, the group should go through the same decision-making steps outlined above. Once the group reaches a conclusion, it needs to work on leading other decision makers through the process in a shortened form so that they can affirm the group's conclusions.

This model of decision making requires both an educational process and access to a variety of information. While a sophisticated and dedicated group of volunteers can use it, a professional often aids in facilitating the process and assembling expert input. When a rabbi does this in a congregational setting, the rabbi can often play a critical role in successful decision making. This requires differentiating among three functions:

- facilitation that creates safety for open inquiry and exchanges of views;
- teaching about Jewish sources and providing other insights;
- stating personal values, reasoning and conclusions.

When these functions are suitably differentiated and labeled, the rabbi can successfully play a central role in an effective process. When the rabbi does not differentiate among the factors, this can fuel interpersonal conflict, disrupt decision making, and prevent the emergence of a decision that the group will accept. The rabbi's expertise is very much needed. Its exercise requires reflection, self-discipline, and commitment to the values-based decision making process.

## *Negotiating Priorities*

Group conflict often peaks at the stage when members negotiate value priorities. At this stage it is possible to look ahead and see which priorities will lead to which conclusions. This is a time when active listening and facilitation can help build consensus, which is not the same as unanimity. For a consensus to emerge, points of commonality must be discovered and emphasized so that people are willing to move forward despite their differences.

Which decisions should a group make? It first ought to make the decisions needed to mount its core programs and provide for their administration. As it adds to its program, new decisions will have to be made. When congregations start, they typically begin making ideological and ritual decisions and then quickly move on to dealing with financial and structural decisions as well. Before long decisions relating to employment and social action are added to the mix. All of these decisions have moral components.

Communities inevitably need policies and procedures, necessitating frequent decisions. In the open society of the United States, group decisions limiting the freedom of individuals ("Who are you to tell me what to do?") are usually accepted only to the extent that they are needed for aspects of group life that the individuals seek. Thus we make decisions about whether the synagogue will have a kosher kitchen or avoid Styrofoam products, but those decisions are not binding on synagogue members when they go home.

## *Shaping Conduct*

One of the major benefits of values-based decision making can be consensus-building and establishing shared group behavior. This in turn shapes the moral conduct of the members of the group. Research shows that most people conform to the attitudes and behaviors of the groups they are in. Thus groups using values-based decision making both provide a model for personal decision-making and reinforce the moral conduct of their members.

If a Reconstructionist congregation has as one of its goals shaping the personal conduct of its members, it will use a broadly inclusive process to produce guidelines for personal conduct - but will not enforce them as rules unless the rules are needed for the welfare of the congregation. This situation results from the fact that today congregations are voluntaristic communities that require the consent of their members. Their health and legitimacy requires that they validate their activities through the consent of their members and act no more coercively than needed to fulfill their agreed-upon purposes.

## *Living Lives of Transcendant Meaning*

In our post-modern world, we know that no one group has the sole claim on justice or ethics. But creating a way of living that we share with our community, a way of living shaped by our attitudes and beliefs, norms and values, allows us to live morally coherent, meaningful lives. When our lives are lived in harmony with the rhythms of our Jewish community, we are reinforced in our morality. If that morality includes attention to improving our world, as authentic Jewish morality must, then it has value that extends beyond our own lives. It brings us to living lives of transcendent meaning.

# INDEX

additives, 39
*ahava*, 15
American Reform Responsa, 13
*anava*, 15
animals, 25, 26, 29, 31, 34
*avadim hayinu bemitzrayim*, 15
*avodah*, 15
avoiding waste, 16
awe of God, 25
baked goods, 39, 46
*bal tashhit*, 12, 16, 32, 33, 42
*basari*, 39
*batel beshishim*, 42
beer, 47
"Be fruitful and multiply.", 22
*b'riyut*, 16
Bialik, Hayim Nachman, 37
*birkhot nehenin*, 22
*bitul z'man*, 16
blessings over food, 35
blood, 29, 30, 44, 45
body image, 28
*brit*, 16
butter, 39
*b'tzelem Elohim*, 15, 17, 23
celebration, 24
cheese, 39, 42, 43
community, 11, 12, 20, 21, 23, 24, 28, 36, 37, 38
connection to God, 17
conspicuous consumption, 33
covenant, 16
covenanted caring, 18
compassion, 23
dairy, 38, 39, 46
dairy additives, 46
*darkhey shalom*, 17
democracy, 12, 17, 22
*d'veykut*, 17
dishes, 32, 40, 41, 42
diversity, 17
do's and don'ts, 11
Douglas, Mary, 29
Earth belongs to God., 20
eco-*kashrut*, 32, 33, 37, 47
egalitarianism, 12, 17, 37
eggs, 39, 42
environment, 18, 24, 32
*emet*, 18
*Eretz Yisrael*, 18, 47
fertility rites, 34
fidelity, 18
fins and scales, 43
fish, 39, 43
*fleishik*, 39, 40
fowl, 44
fruit, 39, 42
gelatin, 46
*glatt* kosher, 44
grains, 39, 42
guarding speech, 24
gratitude, 19, 35, 48
*haganat hateva*, 18, 32, 42

*hakhnasat orhim*, 37
*halakha*, 12, 13, 30, 31, 33, 38
*halal*, 34
*halavi*, 39
*hashgaha*, 42, 46
*havdala*, 11
health, 16, 28, 29
*heksher*, 43, 44, 46, 47
*hesed*, 18
*hidur mitzvah*, 19, 38
*hodaya*, 19, 35
holiness, 19, 24, 28, 30, 35
homosexual, 17
humans in God's image, 16
humility, 15
hunting, 33
improving the world, 24
inclusion, 19
intention, 19
Israel, land of, 18
Jewish authenticity, 19
Jewish civilization, 11, 14, 21, 22, 23
Jewish learning, 21
Judaism as a civilization, 20
Kaplan, Mordecai, 12
*kasher*, 26
*kashrut*, 11, 12, 14, 26-48
*kavana*, 19
*kedusha*, 19, 20, 28, 30, 35
*kehila*, 20
*kiddush*, 47
*Klal Yisrael*, 20, 37
Klein, Isaac, 13
kosher, 26, 33, 35, 36, 37
kosher certification, 46
kosher, *glatt*, 44
kosher kitchen, 37, 38, 40-42
kosher salt, 45
kosher slaughtering, 27, 30, 31, 33, 44
*ladonay ha'aretz umelo'o*, 20
*limud torah*, 21, 36
love, 15
*mashgiah*, 47
Mazon-A Jewish Response to Hunger, 33
Maimonides, Moses (Rambam), 30, 35
meat, 32, 34, 39, 40, 42, 43, 45
*menschlichkeit*, 21
*menuha*, 21
mercy, 23
*minhag*, 40
*mitzvah/ot*, 14, 20, 21, 22
*milchik*, 39, 40, 46
*Mishneh Berura*, 13
modesty, 25
neutral, 39
Noahide laws, 30, 35
obligation, 21
*pareve*, 39, 40, 43, 46, 47
Passover, 41, 47
peace, 17, 23
permitted foods, 42
Philo of Alexandria, 43
physical pleasure, 22

pluralism, 22, 37
preserving chain of tradition, 23, 36
protecting the body, 23
post-*halakhic*, 13
pots and pans, 30, 34, 35, 40
poultry, 32, 34, 44, 45
*p'ru ur'vu,* 22
processed foods, 45
rabbinic supervision, 42
race, 19
*ra<u>h</u>manut*, 23
Rav, 26
Reconstructionist, 13
reinterpretation, 11
renewal, 11, 21
rennet, 42, 43, 46
rest, 21
salting meat, 29, 45
separation of milk and meat, 27, 29, 30, 34, 39
service, 15
sexual orientation, 19
*Shabbat*, 11, 12, 21, 24, 28, 38
Shachter-Shalomi, Zalman, 33
*shalshelet hakabbala*, 23, 36
*she<u>h</u>ita*, 33, 43, 44
*shekhina*, 28
shellfish, 26, 43
*sh'lom bayit*, 23
*sh'mirat haguf*, 23
*sh'mirat halashon,* 24
shortening, 46
*Shul<u>h</u>an Arukh,* 13
*sim<u>h</u>a*, 24
social justice, 25
sodium caseinate, 39, 40
spices, 42
spirituality, 24
sugar, 42
*tikun olam*, 24, 32
*treyf*, 30, 33
truth, 18
*tz'niyut*, 25
*tza'ar ba'aley <u>h</u>ayim,* 25, 31, 32
*tzedek*, 25, 33
*tzedaka*, 25
unity and survival of Jewish people, 20
unity of purpose, 11
utensils, 32, 40, 41
values, 12, 13, 14, 22, 36, 39, 47
*va'ad hakashrut*, 33
vegetables, 42
vegetarian, 31, 32, 38, 47
Waskow, Arthur, 33
wasting time, 16
"We were slaves in Egypt.", 15
whiskey, 47
wine, 26, 47
women and kashrut, 37
*yirat Shamayim*, 25